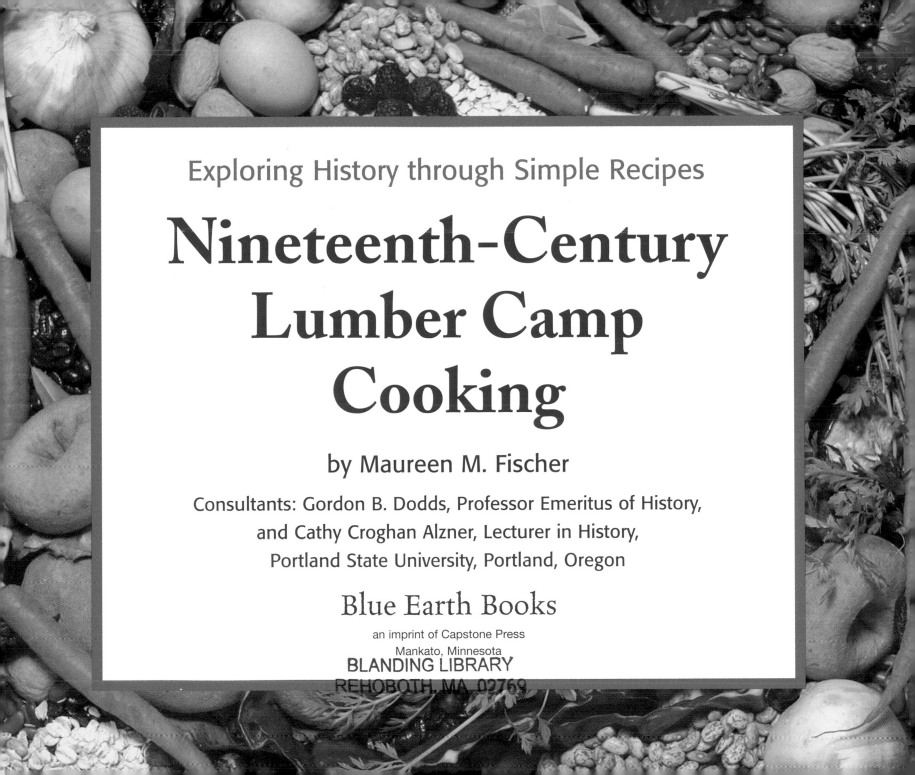

Exploring History through Simple Recipes

Nineteenth-Century Lumber Camp Cooking

by Maureen M. Fischer

Consultants: Gordon B. Dodds, Professor Emeritus of History,
and Cathy Croghan Alzner, Lecturer in History,
Portland State University, Portland, Oregon

Blue Earth Books

an imprint of Capstone Press
Mankato, Minnesota

Blue Earth Books are published by Capstone Press
151 Good Counsel Drive, P.O. Box 669, Mankato, Minnesota 56002
http://www.capstone-press.com

Library of Congress Cataloging-in-Publication Data
Fischer, Maureen M.
 Nineteenth-Century Lumber Camp Cooking / by Maureen M. Fischer.
 p. cm.—(Exploring history through simple recipes)
 Summary: Discusses the everyday life, cooking methods, and common foods eaten by lumberjacks and loggers working in the American West during the nineteenth century. Includes recipes.
 ISBN 0-7368-0604-0
 1. Cookery, American—Western style—Juvenile literature. [1. Food habits—West (U.S.)—History—19th century. 2. Logging—History.] I. Title. II. Series.
TX715.2.W47 F57 2001
641.5978—dc21
                                                                                          00-36769

Editorial credits
Editors, Kay M. Olson, Kerry A. Graves; cover designer, Steve Christensen; cover production and interior designer, Heather Kindseth; illustrator, Linda Clavel; photo researcher, Katy Kudela

Editor's note
Adult supervision may be needed for some recipes in this book. All recipes have been tested. Although based on historical foods, recipes have been modernized and simplified for today's young cooks.

1 2 3 4 5 6 06 05 04 03 02 01

Photo credits
Minnesota Historical Society, cover, 9; Gregg Andersen, cover background, 11, 15, 17, 19 (top), 25, 29; Washington State Historical Society, 7; University of Wisconsin–LaCrosse, 12; Oregon Historical Society, 10, 16, 20, 24; Idaho State Historical Society, 13; North Wind Picture Archives, 8, 22, 26, 28; Washington State University Historical Photograph Collection, 18-19; Library of Congress, 21

Acknowledgements
Blue Earth Books thanks Mary Gunderson for providing the recipes on pages 14 and 15.

Contents

Cooking Help

Recipes

References

Metric Conversion Guide

U.S.	Canada
¼ teaspoon	1 mL
½ teaspoon	2 mL
1 teaspoon	5 mL
1 tablespoon	15 mL
¼ cup	50 mL
⅓ cup	75 mL
½ cup	125 mL
⅔ cup	150 mL
¾ cup	175 mL
1 cup	250 mL
1 quart	1 liter
1 ounce	30 grams
2 ounces	55 grams
4 ounces	85 grams
½ pound	225 grams
1 pound	455 grams

Fahrenheit	Celsius
325 degrees	160 degrees
350 degrees	180 degrees
375 degrees	190 degrees
400 degrees	200 degrees
425 degrees	220 degrees

Kitchen Safety

1. Make sure your hair and clothes will not be in the way while you are cooking.

2. Keep a fire extinguisher in the kitchen. Never put water on a grease fire.

3. Wash your hands with soap before you start to cook. Wash your hands with soap again after you handle meat or poultry.

4. Ask an adult for help with sharp knives, the stove, the oven, and all electrical appliances.

5. Turn handles of pots and pans to the middle of the stove. A person walking by could run into handles that stick out toward the room.

6. Use dry pot holders to take dishes out of the oven.

7. Wash all fruits and vegetables.

8. Always use a clean cutting board. Wash the cutting board thoroughly after cutting meat or poultry.

9. Wipe up spills immediately.

10. Store leftovers properly. Do not leave leftovers out at room temperature for more than two hours.

Cooking Equipment

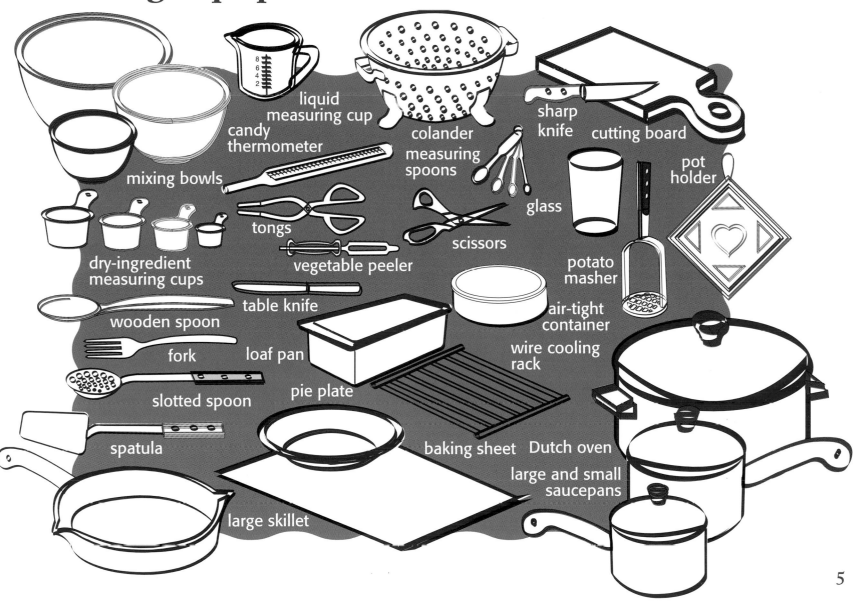

liquid measuring cup

candy thermometer

mixing bowls

colander

measuring spoons

sharp knife

cutting board

pot holder

glass

dry-ingredient measuring cups

tongs

vegetable peeler

scissors

potato masher

table knife

wooden spoon

air-tight container

fork

loaf pan

wire cooling rack

slotted spoon

pie plate

spatula

baking sheet

Dutch oven

large and small saucepans

large skillet

The Logging Boom

North American logging began along the Atlantic coast in the 1600s. Colonists chopped down trees with axes to clear their land for farms. As early as 1700, colonists exported lumber to England and the West Indies. By the 1830s, loggers had cleared most of the huge trees in eastern regions. Loggers moved west to forests near the Great Lakes in Canada and in the United States. By the 1850s, the North American logging industry stretched to the Pacific coast.

During the mid-1800s, pioneers traveled west from the eastern United States. Many followed the Oregon Trail in search of land. Others came to find gold. These new settlers needed lumber to build new farmhouses and towns. The few mills on the West Coast could not provide enough lumber, and eastern lumber was expensive.

The local demand created a logging boom in the Pacific Northwest, where thick forests covered the land. New companies built mills along the Pacific Coast and on inland rivers. Men called "timber cruisers" searched mountain ranges for the best trees. Logging companies bought land or purchased cheaper "stumpage" rights to cut trees on other people's property.

The logging companies hired 12-man crews to fell trees. The men cut down trees during the warmer, dryer months from spring until fall. They delivered their logs to mills, where the logs were cut into boards for sale in Hawaii, Mexico, South America, Asia, and Australia.

As local demand and lumber exports increased, crews with hundreds of loggers became common. Companies hired eastern loggers, failed gold miners, or unhappy sailors at employment offices in cities. Loggers also moved between camps, looking for better food or pay.

Loggers cut huge redwoods, firs, cedars, spruce, and pines in the mountains and along the Pacific Northwest coast, where rain is plentiful. Western trees like the redwoods and Douglas firs are much larger and produce more lumber than eastern trees. Douglas firs sometimes stretch 250 to 300 feet (75 to 90 meters) tall, and are 10 feet (3 meters) in diameter. Redwoods sometimes reach 350 feet (105 meters) and can measure 15 feet (5 meters) in diameter around the base.

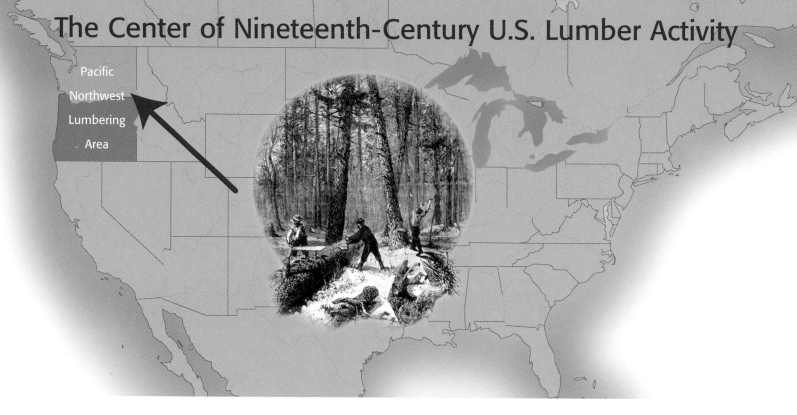

The Center of Nineteenth-Century U.S. Lumber Activity

Pacific Northwest Lumbering Area

Loggers had to be strong and physically fit to do the dangerous work of felling trees. Most of the men were bachelors, because it was difficult for loggers to marry and raise a family while they worked in the woods. Crews worked 10-hour shifts in all types of weather to supply logs for the growing lumber market. Some loggers spent up to six months away from town.

Loggers lived deep in the woods in primitive lumber camps. There were two types of lumber camps. Base camps were the main camps, with a mill, bunkhouse, blacksmith shop, barn, and wanigan. Men received their wages and bought clothes and supplies at wanigans. As loggers cut all the trees around the base camps, they moved deeper into the woods. They built additional lumber camps there. These camps did not have a mill, so logs were moved to the base camp to be cut into lumber. To the loggers, the most important building in any camp was the cookhouse.

Logging Terms and Superstitions

Loggers came from many nations such as Norway, Sweden, Finland, Germany, Italy, and Ireland. There also were Canadian, Chinese, Japanese, Greek, and Native American loggers who worked together in the camps. Because they often could not communicate easily, loggers created their own language.

Some logging expressions have carried over today. The term "skid road" has been shortened to skid row, and describes a rundown area similar to the skid roads in logging areas. When people are in a troublesome spot they are said to be "in a jam," much like loggers who had to clear blocked logs from rivers. Loggers often used wire from hay bales to fix anything in camp that was broken. People still describe things that are not working as being "haywire."

Many loggers had superstitions that they shared with each other. They believed a logger who sharpened his ax on Sunday would cut himself on Monday. Men never slept with their head downstream on a river drive, believing someone would drown. Starting to cut a new area on Friday was bad luck. Some believed that if a fat logger arrived in camp, it meant three accidents would happen.

9

The Cook and the Cookhouse

A good cook was the pride of the camp. After the foreman, he was the most important crew member. Many loggers chose a camp by the cook and the quality of the food he served. If the cook's food tasted bad or his servings were small, loggers quit and moved on to another camp. These bellyrobber cooks were quickly replaced.

A cook supervised his assistants. Flunkies did all the dirty, boring jobs that the cook did not want to do. They washed dishes, peeled potatoes, set tables, and swept the floor. At mealtimes, they refilled serving dishes, milk pitchers, and coffee pots. Afterward, they cleared the tables. The bull cook was another assistant. His first job was to feed the oxen. He also chopped firewood and hauled water. Cooks worked about 15 hours a day, even on Sunday.

Cooking methods for lumber camp cooks were primitive in the mid-1800s. The cook worked at an open fire located in the center of the bunkhouse. The cook hung kettles over the fire or placed iron pots in the coals to prepare food. In the late 1800s, cooks switched to wood stoves. Cooking on a stove was easier. Stove pipes ran up through the roof to keep the bunkhouse clear of smoke.

As crews grew, the cookhouse moved to a separate building. Long tables and benches where the men ate filled most of the room. The kitchen area with the stove and work tables was at one end of the building. Cooks stored iron pans on ceiling hooks or on shelves. Clean dishes and silverware did not need to be stored in cupboards.

Until World War I (1914–1918), most cooks and flunkies in lumber camps were men. Occasionally, the wife of a foreman worked as a cook.

Corned Beef and Boiled Potatoes

Ingredients	Equipment
3-pound corned beef with seasoning packet	Dutch oven with lid
water	scissors
6 medium potatoes	cutting board
6 carrots	sharp knife
	fork
	vegetable peeler
	slotted spoon

1. Remove seasoning packet from corned beef.
2. Place meat in Dutch oven. Open seasoning packet with scissors and sprinkle seasoning over meat.
3. Add enough water into the Dutch oven to cover the corned beef. Bring to a boil.
4. Reduce heat. Cover and simmer 3 hours or until meat is tender.
5. Peel potatoes and carrots. Cut potatoes and carrots in half crosswise.
6. Add potatoes and carrots to Dutch oven. Cover and cook 30 minutes or until vegetables are tender.
7. Remove meat to cutting board and cut into slices ½ to 1 inch thick (1.5 to 2.5 centimeters) thick. Use slotted spoon to remove vegetables.

Makes 6 to 8 servings

The flunkies set the tables again after each meal. The cook stored food in a pantry or root cellar. Some camps had a separate smokehouse for salt pork, smoked fish, and cured corned beef, called red horse. Smokehouses were locked to keep animals from stealing the food.

Cooks bought foods in barrels from distant towns. They ordered foods that did not spoil quickly, such as rice, flour, beans, potatoes, and dried fruit. They sweetened food with maple syrup or molasses. Fresh foods were rare unless loggers hunted, fished, or picked berries. In later years, cooks bought milk and vegetables from nearby settlers. They also kept pigs to eat kitchen scraps and to provide fresh pork.

Early to Bed, Early to Rise

Morning activities began very early in lumber camps. The cook and flunkies woke up at about 4 a.m. to prepare breakfast. They were the first men up in camp. A logger's day started between 4:30 a.m. and 5 a.m. with the wake-up call of "daylight in the swamp" or "roll out or roll up." Some loggers washed quickly with soap and cold water. They all dressed in long underwear, wool shirts, "tin" pants rubbed with grease or pitch to make them waterproof, and suspenders. They could not wear their corked (KAWKD) boots in the cookhouse. The metal spikes on the bottom of the boots helped the loggers remain steady on wet logs, but damaged the cookhouse floors.

Hungry and barely awake, the loggers started heading to the dining hall for breakfast around 5:30 a.m. The meal was quick, but hearty. Men devoured stacks of pancakes, fried eggs, biscuits, bacon, ham, fried potatoes, doughnuts, and pots of steaming coffee or tea. Loggers were allowed to eat as much as they wanted. They needed a lot of energy for a full day of work.

At 6 a.m. the foreman yelled, "All out for the woods." The loggers left the cookhouse and put on their corked boots. They gathered their equipment and headed for the choppings where they cut trees. Each logger carried a two-headed ax, an 8-foot (2.5-meter) crosscut saw, an oil bottle, a 4-foot (1.2-meter) springboard, wedges, and a sledgehammer to work every day. They needed all these tools to do their job in the woods.

At half past four in the morning, the flunkies set the tables and mixed a couple pailsful of half powdered skim milk and half canned milk. They rang the wake-up bell at 5:30 a.m., half an hour before breakfast. They then got out of the way of the hungry loggers who came running in for breakfast.

13

Sourdough Starter

Make sourdough starter one or two days before pancakes.

Ingredients
2 cups warm water,
     105°F to 115°F
     (40°C to 46°C)
1 package active dry yeast
     (2¼ teaspoons)
2 cups all-purpose flour

Equipment
liquid measuring cup
candy thermometer
large bowl
wooden spoon
dry-ingredient measuring
     cups
plastic wrap
air-tight container

1. Heat 2 cups water in microwave for 1 minute. Test temperature with candy thermometer. Water should be about 110°F (43°C). If water is too cool, heat in microwave again for 15 seconds. If water is too hot, set it aside to cool to correct temperature.
2. Pour warm water into large bowl. Dissolve yeast in warm water. Let stand about 10 minutes until mixture is bubbly.
3. Gradually add 2 cups flour to water, stirring often.
4. Cover bowl loosely with plastic wrap.
5. Let stand at room temperature 24 to 48 hours, stirring occasionally.

Refrigerate sourdough starter in an air-tight container.

Dangerous Duties

Loggers never knew if they would return safely to camp each night. Just carrying sharp saws and axes could be dangerous if a logger tripped in the brush. Loggers cut off their pants above the top of their boots to avoid tripping.

Even river drivers who could swim faced the possibility of drowning. Their heavily corked boots made loggers sink if they fell off logs.

All loggers feared forest fires. Fires moved quickly on the hillside forests, which made it difficult for loggers to reach safety.

As technology improved, dangers increased. Mechanical saws buzzed so quickly, a mill worker could cut himself in an instant. Locomotives carrying logs on a steep slope could go out of control and crash. Rickety trestles sometimes collapsed under the weight of heavy logs.

By the 1880s, loggers used mechanical cable winches called steam donkeys to move logs on hillsides. These machines were powered by steam boilers. The fire fueling the steam donkey sometimes got too hot and the boiler exploded. Nearby loggers could be burned by the hot water spraying from an exploding boiler.

Sourdough Pancakes

These pancakes have a rich, tangy flavor. You need sourdough starter to make this recipe. Make the sourdough starter at least two days before you plan to make sourdough pancakes.

Ingredients

The night before making pancakes:
2 cups sourdough starter
1 cup all-purpose flour
1 cup warm (tap) water or warm milk
2 tablespoons firmly packed brown sugar
½ teaspoon salt

The day you make pancakes:
2 tablespoons vegetable oil
1 teaspoon baking soda
2 eggs
1 tablespoon vegetable oil for frying

Equipment
large bowl
wooden spoon
dry-ingredient measuring cups
liquid measuring cup
measuring spoons
plastic wrap
skillet or electric frying pan
spatula
air-tight container (optional)

The Night Before:

1. In large bowl, mix 2 cups sourdough starter, 1 cup flour, 1 cup water, 2 tablespoons brown sugar, and ½ teaspoon salt until well blended.
2. Cover the sourdough loosely with plastic wrap and let stand at room temperature.

The Next Morning:

1. Measure out 2 cups sourdough and place in large bowl. Discard remaining sourdough or place it in an air-tight container and refrigerate for later use.
2. Add 2 tablespoons vegetable oil and 1 teaspoon baking soda to sourdough in bowl. Stir 2 eggs into the batter.
3. Heat 1 tablespoon oil in skillet or electric frying pan.
4. Pour ⅛-cup portions of batter into hot skillet. Cook until dry around edges and bubbly all over. Turn and cook another 2 minutes.
5. Serve immediately with butter, syrup, jam, or honey.

Makes 18 to 22 pancakes

"Pass the Bread" and Other Rules

Logging was risky, so rules were strict. Loggers who did not follow orders were fired. In the woods, men shouted "timber" to warn others of a falling tree. Many loggers were hurt or killed by trees and logs that landed on them. Loggers warned others when falling branches snapped off a tree. As these "widowmakers" fell, they could instantly kill a man. Loggers looked around them before swinging an ax. A man could quickly bleed to death from an ax cut.

In most camps, alcohol and gambling were not allowed. Men who lived in such close quarters could have short tempers. Drunk loggers easily got into arguments or fights. The foreman stopped fights with warnings, then with his fists.

Each night in camp, the men inspected their tools. The company owned the tools, but the loggers cleaned, sharpened, and repaired them. As lumber crews grew, men were hired to do all the repair work and blade sharpening for the entire camp. Tools had to be in good condition. Broken handles or dull blades could cause injuries.

In the cookhouse, the cook made the rules. He assigned each logger a permanent spot at the table. The men could find their seats and eat more quickly that way. Talking was not allowed during meals, except to say things such as "pass the bread" or "shoot the beans" for a second helping. Conversation delayed the men in heading to work. The cook gave disorderly loggers a blow from a frying pan, a serving utensil, or firewood. Loggers who did not behave were kicked out of the cookhouse. They learned to follow the rules after missing a meal.

Loggers stood on springboards while swinging sharp axes. For their own safety, the men had to obey the strict rules of the lumber camp.

Oatmeal Bread

Ingredients
2 cups all-purpose flour
1 package active dry yeast
1⅓ cups water
⅓ cup honey
2 tablespoons margarine or butter
1 teaspoon salt
2 cups rolled oats
2½ cups all-purpose flour
3 tablespoons shortening for
 greasing

Equipment
2 large bowls
liquid measuring cup
dry-ingredient measuring cups
measuring spoons
medium saucepan
wooden spoon
paper towel or napkin
two 8-inch (20-centimeter)
 loaf pans
clean kitchen towel
pot holders
wire cooling rack

1. In bowl, mix 2 cups flour and yeast.
2. In saucepan over medium heat, cook and stir 1⅓ cups water, ⅓ cup honey, 2 tablespoons margarine or butter, and 1 teaspoon salt until butter is almost melted.
3. Add contents of saucepan to flour and yeast mixture. With a wooden spoon, beat mixture until it is smooth.
4. Stir in 2 cups rolled oats and 2 to 2½ cups of flour.
5. Place dough on a lightly floured surface and knead in enough of the remaining flour to make a stiff dough. Knead by pushing the dough with the heels of your palm, fold, and repeat. Knead 6 to 8 minutes, until the dough is smooth.
6. Use a paper towel or napkin dabbed with shortening to grease insides of large bowl and loaf pans.
7. Shape dough into a ball and place in the greased bowl. Cover with clean towel and let rise in warm place about 1 hour or until it doubles in size.
8. With your fist, punch down dough and let it stand 10 minutes.
9. Divide dough and place into greased loaf pans. Cover with clean towel and let rise in warm place about 1 hour or until it is double in size.
10. Preheat oven to 375°F. Bake 35 to 40 minutes.
11. Remove bread onto wire cooling rack.

Makes 2 loaves

Out in the Woods

Loggers faced many difficulties on the job. Bases of huge western trees were too wide to go through the mill saws. The base also was full of sticky pitch that made the wood hard to cut. To solve these problems, loggers called fallers cut notches in the trees about 4 feet (1.2 meters) off the ground, where the tree was narrower. They inserted a springboard into the notch. An iron hook on the end held the board steady. Loggers stood on the springboard to chop.

Many men with different jobs worked to cut down a single tree. In the 1870s, pairs of loggers used double-bladed axes to notch and chop trees. The notch was cut on the side the loggers wanted the tree to land. Fallers chopped a backcut toward the notch from the opposite side of the tree. In the 1880s, fallers began to use crosscut saws for the backcut, which was much quicker. Fallers cut twice as many trees each day using saws. A logger called a bucker then sawed the tree into smaller logs. Other men chained one end of the log to a two-wheeled wagon. Oxen pulled the wagons to drag the logs over the brush to a cleared yard.

By noon the loggers were ravenous. Men who worked far from camp brought their lunches. These nosebags contained cold sandwiches, hard-boiled eggs, and cake. Men made tea or coffee over a fire. If the men were near camp, they could return to the cookhouse. Usually a flunky brought hot lunch out to the choppings on a swingdingle. He loaded this ox-drawn cart with hot sandwiches, potatoes and gravy, and pie. The flunky wrapped blankets around the pots to keep the food hot. Loggers sat on stumps and logs to eat. After lunch, the loggers went back to work while the flunky cleaned up and returned to camp.

Some loggers carried their lunches in little canvas bags. In other camps, flunkies brought a hot lunch out to the choppings.

Hot Roast Beef Sandwiches

Serve hot roast beef sandwiches on oatmeal bread (page 17) with mashed potatoes and gravy (page 23).

Ingredients
¼ cup all-purpose flour
½ teaspoon salt
¼ teaspoon pepper
3-pound boneless beef rump roast
1 tablespoon vegetable oil
2 cups water
1 large onion
¼ cup water
6 slices bread

Equipment
small bowl
dry-ingredient measuring cups
measuring spoons
wooden spoon
sharp knife
Dutch oven and lid
fork
liquid measuring cup
cutting board
small container

1. In small bowl, mix ¼ cup flour, ½ teaspoon salt and ¼ teaspoon pepper; stir. Use your fingers to rub mixture into rump roast.
2. Heat oil in Dutch oven over medium high heat until hot. Add roast and brown on all sides, using a fork to turn the roast.
3. Add 2 cups water. Reduce heat. Cover and simmer 1½ hours.
4. Peel onion and cut into slices. Cut slices in half.
5. Add onion. If necessary, add ¼ cup water to keep roast moist. Cook covered 1 hour more or until beef is soft when poked with a fork.
6. Carefully remove beef from Dutch oven and place on cutting board.
7. Using a wooden spoon, skim fat from juices. Save juices in small container for gravy (page 23).
8. Cut meat into slices. Place on top of bread slices.

Makes 6 to 8 servings

From Logs to Lumber

The logs piled in the yard were still a long distance from the mill. To transport them, hooktenders first peeled bark off the bottom of the logs and connected them with chains. Six or more logs together made up a turn. Ten or 12 oxen pulled the turn onto the 8-foot-wide (2.5-meter-wide) skid road. Men placed logs called skids 6 feet (2 meters) apart to make the surface of this trail. Skid roads led from the yard and down the mountain. A skid greaser swabbed the skids with fish oil, bear grease, or spoiled butter to help the logs slide.

The bull whacker guided the oxen down the skid road. Controlling these slow, strong animals often was difficult. At the bottom of the skid road, men loaded logs onto ox-carts or into a river to carry or float them to the sawmills. By the 1890s, loggers had replaced oxen with horses because they were faster and easier to train. During winter, logs could be pulled over ice and snow in the mountains without a skid road.

By the 1890s, loggers had replaced oxen with horses to pull the logs down the skid roads. Horses were faster and easier to train than oxen. At the bottom of the skid road, men loaded the logs onto flatbed train cars or carried them to a river to float them to the sawmills.

Loggers sometimes sent the logs down a mountain slope by way of nearby rivers or streams.

20

21

Chutes transported logs down steep slopes where skid roads could not be built. These long wooden troughs stretched from the yard down the mountain. Greased logs slid down the chute.

If streams were close by, loggers diverted water into the chute to float logs quickly down the mountain. Loggers called watered chutes flumes. They dared each other to ride a log down the rushing water flume. Only the bravest loggers took this challenge.

Loggers used nearby streams to float logs to the sawmills. During spring, melting snow made large rivers run high and fast. In smaller streams, loggers built splash dams. These wooden barriers reserved water until there was enough to float the logs.

Loggers called river dogs steered logs and kept them from piling up into a log jam. River dogs had to balance, walk, and jump on the floating, rolling logs. This talent was called birling. If the logs jammed, the men loosened them with long hooked poles called peaveys. Tough jams had to be blown loose with dynamite. River dogs had one of the most dangerous jobs in logging.

If there were no rivers large enough to float the logs to the base camp sawmill, men loaded logs onto carts at the bottom of the skid roads and flumes. When they reached the sawmill, the huge trees were cut into boards. The most basic type of mill was the whipsaw mill, where two men used a double-handled saw to cut boards by hand. Other early mills were built next to rivers, where the running water pushed a large paddlewheel. The paddlewheel turned a gearshaft that powered the saw blades inside the mill. The first steam-powered sawmill was built in 1844. This technology spread quickly because steam saws could cut boards faster and make more money for logging companies.

River dogs followed orders from the driver who spotted a key log that started the logjam. Loggers used poles, axes, and other tools to pry loose jammed logs on the river.

Mashed Potatoes and Gravy

Ingredients

For potatoes:
2 pounds potatoes
  (about 6 medium)
1 teaspoon salt
water (to cover potatoes)
½ cup milk
2 tablespoons margarine or
  butter

¼ teaspoon salt
For gravy:
saved juices from pot roast
  (or 2 cups beef broth)
2 tablespoons all-purpose flour
2 tablespoons water
½ teaspoon salt
¼ teaspoon pepper

Equipment

For potatoes:
vegetable peeler
knife
cutting board
large saucepan and lid
measuring spoons
colander
large bowl

potato masher
liquid measuring cup
For gravy:
liquid measuring cup
medium saucepan
small bowl
measuring spoons
wooden spoon

For potatoes:
1. With vegetable peeler, peel 6 medium potatoes. With knife, cut potatoes into quarters on cutting board.
2. Place potato quarters and 1 teaspoon salt in large saucepan. Cover potatoes with water.
3. Bring water to a boil over medium heat; cover.
4. Cook 25 to 30 minutes.
5. Carefully drain potatoes in colander.
6. Place potatoes in large bowl. Use potato masher to mash hot potatoes until there are no lumps.
7. In medium saucepan, heat ½ cup milk, 2 tablespoons margarine, and ¼ teaspoon salt until butter or margarine is melted.

8. Add milk mixture to potatoes and beat with potato masher until potatoes are light and fluffy.

For gravy:
1. Measure out juices from roast. If necessary, add enough water so liquid equals 2 cups.
2. Put juices in medium saucepan.
3. In small bowl, mix 2 tablespoons each flour and water, ½ teaspoon salt, and ¼ teaspoon pepper; stir.
4. Add dry ingredients to saucepan. Bring to a boil over medium heat, stirring constantly, until gravy is thickened.

Makes 6 to 8 servings

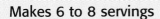

23

Back to Camp

After logging until dark, men were hungry, tired, and wet. In summer, they sweated in the heat. From fall to spring, the men worked in the rain or snow. They returned to the bunkhouse to change their boots, wet or sweaty socks, and long underwear, which they wore year-round. The loggers hung these clothes over bunkhouse rafters, ends of a bed, or the deacon's bench, a long seat made from split logs. The men then washed up and headed for the cookhouse.

Each night the men expected a hearty supper of meat, rice or potatoes, and bread or biscuits. The cook sometimes fixed stew or soup. Loggers ate beans at every meal because they were cheap, easy to store, filling, and tasty. Dessert included cakes, cookies, and pies.

After supper, the men went to the bunkhouse. The bunkhouse was a one-room shanty. The 40 foot-long (12 meter-long) building was made from logs or rough-cut boards. Mud and moss sealed out drafts between the logs. The bunkhouse did not have windows because it was usually dark when the men were in camp. Water barrels or washing troughs usually stood outside the door.

In 1897, many lumber camps looked like this one on the banks of the Columbia River in Washington.

Raisin Pie

Ingredients

1 package refrigerated
  pie crusts
2 cups raisins
1½ cups water
½ cup packed brown sugar
2 tablespoons all-purpose
  flour
½ cup chopped walnuts
2 tablespoons margarine
  or butter
1 tablespoon cider vinegar

Equipment

medium saucepan
dry-ingredient measuring
  cups
liquid measuring cup
wooden spoon
measuring spoons
table knife
9-inch (23-centimeter)
  pie plate
pot holders
fork

1. Remove pie crusts from refrigerator.
2. In medium saucepan, mix 2 cups raisins and 1½ cups water. Heat to boiling. Simmer 5 minutes.
3. Add ½ cup brown sugar and 2 tablespoons flour to raisin mixture; stir. Heat to boiling over medium heat, stirring constantly. Cook and stir 1 minute.
4. Remove from heat. Stir in ½ cup chopped walnuts, 2 tablespoons margarine or butter and 1 tablespoon vinegar. Let cool 10 minutes.
5. Place one pastry into pie plate.
6. Pour raisin mixture into the pastry.
7. Cut small slits in the other pastry crust. Cover pie with top crust. Seal edges.
8. Press edges with the back of a fork.
9. Bake in a 425°F oven 25 to 30 minutes.

Makes 8 servings

Bunkhouses were not comfortable. Rows of double or triple bunk beds crowded the walls. The beds were placed so close together that loggers had to climb in from the end. Two men sometimes shared a bunk. Straw or pine needle mattresses often held lice and bedbugs. The bunkhouse smelled like wet socks, wood smoke, tobacco, and lamp oil.

Companies charged loggers up to one-third of their wages for meals and a bed. At the end of each day, the camp clerk recorded each logger's wages in the camp books. Early loggers earned between $1 and $1.50 each day. The cooks and the foreman made between $2 and $2.50. A bull whacker could earn $100 to $150 each month.

Loggers had only a few hours between supper and bedtime. They sharpened their tools using a foot-powered grindstone in the bunkhouse while they talked. Some loggers might play cards or whittle. Others could play instruments and sing songs. Most loggers could not read or write, so few men read books or sent letters home. Lights out in most camps was at 9 p.m.

Many loggers spent evenings swapping stories about their lives, their work, and their heroes. Some stories were true or partly true. Some stories were about real loggers like Jim Stewart, Joe Fournier, or Joe Montferrand. Others were tall tales or made-up stories. The most famous logging tall tales are about Paul Bunyan and his giant blue ox, Babe. Loggers claimed that Paul created the Mississippi River and other geographical landmarks.

Some stories were meant to tease young loggers who had little experience. These greenhorns often believed stories of strange creatures that lived in the woods. They feared the beasts and kept a close lookout while working. The Hodag was said to be a frightening creature with the face of a lion and horns like an ox. He had a spiny back and the tail of a dinosaur. Other beasts the loggers talked about included the shy Tote Road Shagamaw, which had bear claws on its front feet and moose hooves on its back feet. This creature supposedly ate coats and mittens that loggers thought they had lost. The ape-faced Agropelter supposedly lived in the hollow of a tree and threw branches at the men. The Dungarvon Whooper was said to have a long, brown body with a tail and was able to leap 20 feet (6 meters) in one jump. Some loggers claimed that the beast screeched like the devil, but others said they heard only a mountain lion.

Many areas of the United States have statues of the legendary Paul Bunyan. This one faces the Penobscot River in Bangor, Maine.

Split Pea Soup

Ingredients

1 pound dried yellow split peas
 (about 2¼ cups)
8 cups water
1 medium onion
2 medium carrots
1 cup chopped fully cooked ham
1 teaspoon salt
¼ teaspoon pepper
2 bay leaves

Equipment

scissors
colander
vegetable peeler
cutting board
sharp knife
Dutch oven with lid
dry-ingredient measuring cups
measuring spoons
wooden spoon

1. With scissors, open bag of peas. Place peas in a colander. Rinse peas with water and remove any dented or discolored peas.
2. With vegetable peeler, peel carrots. With knife, peel onion. Chop onion and carrots into ½-inch (1-centimeter) pieces.
3. In Dutch oven, mix peas, 8 cups water, chopped carrots, chopped onion, 1 cup chopped ham, 1 teaspoon salt, ¼ teaspoon pepper, and 2 bay leaves and stir.
4. Bring to a boil over medium heat. Reduce heat. Cover and simmer about 1 hour or until soup is thick and peas are soft and tender.
5. With spoon, carefully remove bay leaves and throw them away.

Makes 6 servings

Time Off

Sunday was the loggers' day off. After six days of chopping trees, they had a chance to relax and play. The cook and flunkies did not get a day off. They roasted meats, cooked beans, and baked cookies just as they did every other day of the week.

Because the loggers did not get up early to work on Sunday, the day off usually started on Saturday evening. In camps close to towns, men cleaned up, then walked or rode horses into town. Some had too much to drink in saloons and ended up in fights. These men often were kept in jail overnight. In remote camps, men held their own dances, played cards or dice, talked, and told stories. Someone usually played the harmonica, accordion, or fiddle. Because women did not live in the lumber camps, two men danced together. Loggers took turns wearing flour-sack aprons tied around their waists as skirts. Loggers also arm-wrestled or played games such as blind-man's bluff.

Sunday was wash day for the loggers and their clothes. The men patched holes in their clothes and washed them in wooden tubs or barrels. They hung their clothes on tree branches or shrubs to dry. If it was raining, the loggers could hang their wet clothes in the bunkhouse to dry. Men also took time to bathe on Sundays. They trimmed each other's hair, beards, and mustaches. Some men shaved each week.

Visitors to camp called on Sundays. A traveling minister sometimes made his rounds and held religious services for the loggers who were interested. Visiting photographers recorded the men, their equipment, and pastimes as they lived and worked in the woods.

Molasses Cookies

Ingredients

1 cup sugar
½ cup shortening
1 egg
½ cup molasses
2 cups all-purpose flour
1 teaspoon baking soda
½ teaspoon ground cinnamon
½ teaspoon ground ginger
¼ teaspoon ground cloves
¼ teaspoon salt
sugar

Equipment

medium bowl
dry-ingredient measuring cups
wooden spoon
measuring spoons
plastic wrap
small bowl
baking sheet
glass
pot holders
spatula
wire cooling rack

1. In medium bowl, mix 1 cup sugar and ½ cup shortening. Stir well.
2. Add 1 egg and ½ cup molasses. Stir until combined.
3. Add 2 cups flour, 1 teaspoon baking soda, ½ teaspoon cinnamon, ½ teaspoon ginger, ¼ teaspoon ground cloves, and ¼ teaspoon salt. Stir until well mixed.
4. Cover bowl with plastic wrap. Chill in refrigerator 1 hour.
5. Heat oven to 350°F.
6. Shape dough into 1-inch (2.5-centimeter) balls. Place some sugar in a small bowl. Rolls balls in sugar.
7. Place balls on baking sheet 2 inches (5 centimeters) apart. Flatten each cookie with the bottom of a glass dipped in sugar.
8. Bake 8 to 10 minutes. Remove cookie sheet from oven using pot holders.
9. Using spatula, carefully move cookies to cooling rack.

Makes 36 cookies

Loggers held their own dances, played cards or dice, talked, and told stories on their time off. Someone usually played the harmonica, the accordion, or the fiddle.

Words to Know

bellyrobber (BEL-ee-ROB-uhr)—a cook who prepared poor-quality food

bull cook (BUL KUK)—a cook's assistant who also did odd jobs around the lumber camp

choppings (CHOP-pingz)—the place in the forest where men cut trees

deacon's bench (DEE-kuhnz BENCH)—long benches made from split logs on which the loggers could sit; deacon's benches were kept in the bunkhouse.

flunky (FLUHNG-kee)—cook's helper who helped prepare food, serve, and clean up

greenhorn (GREEN-horn)—a young or new logger

nosebag (NOHZ-bag)—a cold lunch eaten in the woods, or the canvas bag that held the lunch

swingdingle (SWING-DING-guhl)—a sled or cart used to transport lunch to loggers working more than a mile away from camp

wanigan (WAHN-ih-guhn)—a lumber camp store where loggers could buy clothes and personal items

To Learn More

Adams, Peter Dow. *Early Loggers and the Sawmill.* New York: Crabtree Publishing, 1992.

Davis, Wendy. *Douglas Fir.* Habitats. New York: Children's Press, 1997.

Kurelek, William. *Lumberjack.* New York: Tundra Books, 1996.

Nelson, Sharlene and Ted. *Bullwhackers to Whistle Punks: Logging in the Old West.* A First Book. New York: Franklin Watts, 1996.

Stewart, Gail. *Lumbermen.* The Wild West in American History. Vero Beach, Fla.: Rourke, 1990.

Stone, Lynn M. *Timber Country.* Back Roads. Vero Beach, Fla.: Rourke, 1993.

Places to Write and Visit

British Columbia Forest Discovery Center
2892 Drinkwater Road
RR#4, Trans Canada Highway
Duncan, BC V9L 2C6
Canada

Camp Six Logging Museum
Point Defiance Park
Pearl Street
Tacoma, WA 98407

**Collier Memorial State Park
  Logging Museum**
46000 Hwy 97 N
Chiloquin, OR 97624

Coos County Historical Society Museum
1220 Sherman Avenue
North Bend, OR 97459

Whatcom Museum of History and Art
121 Prospect Street
Bellingham, WA 98225

World Forestry Center
4033 SW Canyon Road
Portland, OR 97221

Internet Sites

Camp Six Logging Museum
http://www.ohwy.com/wa/c/camp6lom.htm

Logging History, Sweet Home, Oregon
http://www.sweet-home.or.us/forest/
logging-history/index.html

**Oregon Public Broadcasting,
  The Oregon Story**
http://education.opb.org/learning/oregonstory/
logging

Pacific Northwest Logging History
http://www.aone.com/~robert/histlog.html

Index